water

A GUIDED JOURNAL THROUGH SCRIPTURE

My Word in 30 Days

HILLSEED
JOURNALS

LYNDSEY LINDSAY

COPYRIGHT ©2022 HILLSEED JOURNALS.

All rights reserved. No part of this book may be reproduced in any form without written permission from the publisher. Do not replicate or copy.

ISBN 978-1-7377809-1-5

Scripture quotations taken from the (NASB®) New American Standard Bible®, Copyright ©1960, 1971, 1977, 1995, 2020 by The Lockman Foundation. Used by permission. All rights reserved. www.lockman.org

All images ©Adobe Stock (stock.adobe.com). Used with license.

Copyright ©2011 The Montserrat Project Authors (https://github.com/JulietaUla/Montserrat). Used with permission.

Book cover design by The Book Cover Whisperer: ProfessionalBookCoverDesign.com

HOW TO USE THIS JOURNAL

We are so glad you are here!

The Bible is our most useful tool for getting to know who God is and His purpose for our lives, and we can't wait for you to do both.

The pages ahead are grouped into **three parts**, all designed to gently guide you through scripture and prompt you to **pursue the Holy Spirit in this journey over the next 30 days**.

1 Introduction..5

> Start by uncovering your big picture thoughts and ideas for the 30 days ahead that you will spend in scripture.
>
> You will also find a resource to introduce you to the major themes of the books of the Bible.

2 My Word in 30 Days..11

> Each day will introduce new scripture with consistent and guided journaling prompts.

3 Insights + Action..73

> After digging into *My Word in 30 Days*, you'll put it all together to uncover key biblical insights and faith-based action steps.

Let's grow our understanding of the Bible one day at a time.

For more information and resources:
visit **www.hillseedjournals.com**

introduction

The Lord is my shepherd, I shall not want. He makes me lie down in green pastures; He leads me beside quiet waters.

PSALM 23:1-2

Water is woven in God's story as a powerful symbol throughout the Old and New Testaments.

Over the next 30 days, you will explore how water appears throughout scripture—from Noah's Ark first finding land after the flood that marked a new promise to God's people, to the baptism of Jesus in the Jordan River, to the living water promised to those who believe.

No matter where you are in your faith, we have all experienced times when we open our Bibles and are unsure of where to start or had difficulty understanding scripture.

This is more than a Bible study. This is more than the word "water".

This is about creating confidence to read, reflect, and apply the Word to our lives every day.

WATER

What does water mean to you? Define the full meaning of water in your own words.

What do you want to learn about water over the next 30 days? Share your thoughts and ideas below.

RESOURCE | OLD TESTAMENT BOOK THEMES

LAW
Genesis
Exodus
Leviticus
Numbers
Deuteronomy

HISTORY
Joshua
Judges
Ruth
1 Samuel
2 Samuel
1 Kings
2 Kings
1 Chronicles
2 Chronicles
Ezra
Nehemiah
Esther

WISDOM
Job
Psalms
Proverbs
Ecclesiates
Song of Solomon

PROPHECY
Isaiah
Jeremiah
Lamentations
Ezekiel
Daniel
Hosea
Joel
Amos
Obadiah
Jonah
Micah
Nahum
Habakkuk
Zephaniah
Haggai
Zachariah
Malachi

NEW TESTAMENT BOOK THEMES

GOSPELS
Matthew
Mark
Luke
John

HISTORY
Acts

LETTERS
Romans
1 Corinthians
2 Corinthians
Galatians
Ephesians
Philippians
Colossians
1 Thessalonians
2 Thessalonians
1 Timothy
2 Timothy
Titus
Philemon
Hebrews
James
1 Peter
2 Peter
1 John
2 John
3 John
Jude

PROPHECY
Revelation

> **TIP**: *Use this resource to consider the major themes and context of the books of the Bible.*

my word in 30 days

When you pass through the
waters, I will be with you;
and through the rivers, they
will not overflow you.

ISAIAH 43:2a

DAY 1 | WATER

Pray over today's scripture, asking the Holy Spirit to lead you. Reread it and write what stands out in the space below.

GENESIS 7

Observe the text for context, teaching, and themes.

What is God revealing to you?

How can you apply this to your life today?

Prayer + Notes

DAY 2 | WATER

Pray over today's scripture, asking the Holy Spirit to lead you. Reread it and write what stands out in the space below.

PSALM 65:9-13

Observe the text for context, teaching, and themes.

What is God revealing to you?

How can you apply this to your life today?

Prayer + Notes

DAY 3 | WATER

Pray over today's scripture, asking the Holy Spirit to lead you. Reread it and write what stands out in the space below.

GENESIS 21:9-21

Observe the text for context, teaching, and themes.

What is God revealing to you?

How can you apply this to your life today?

Prayer + Notes

DAY 4 | WATER

Pray over today's scripture, asking the Holy Spirit to lead you. Reread it and write what stands out in the space below.

EXODUS 2:1-10

Observe the text for context, teaching, and themes.

What is God revealing to you?

How can you apply this to your life today?

Prayer + Notes

DAY 5 | WATER

Pray over today's scripture, asking the Holy Spirit to lead you. Reread it and write what stands out in the space below.

EXODUS 14:13-31

Observe the text for context, teaching, and themes.

What is God revealing to you?

How can you apply this to your life today?

Prayer + Notes

DAY 6 | WATER

Pray over today's scripture, asking the Holy Spirit to lead you. Reread it and write what stands out in the space below.

EXODUS 15:22-27

Observe the text for context, teaching, and themes.

What is God revealing to you?

How can you apply this to your life today?

Prayer + Notes

DAY 7 | WATER

Pray over today's scripture, asking the Holy Spirit to lead you. Reread it and write what stands out in the space below.

EXODUS 17:1-7

Observe the text for context, teaching, and themes.

What is God revealing to you?

How can you apply this to your life today?

Prayer + Notes

DAY 8 | WATER

Pray over today's scripture, asking the Holy Spirit to lead you. Reread it and write what stands out in the space below.

JOSHUA 3

Observe the text for context, teaching, and themes.

What is God revealing to you?

How can you apply this to your life today?

Prayer + Notes

DAY 9 | WATER

Pray over today's scripture, asking the Holy Spirit to lead you. Reread it and write what stands out in the space below.

JOSHUA 4

Observe the text for context, teaching, and themes.

What is God revealing to you?

How can you apply this to your life today?

Prayer + Notes

DAY 10 | WATER

Pray over today's scripture, asking the Holy Spirit to lead you. Reread it and write what stands out in the space below.

2 KINGS 2:1-14

Observe the text for context, teaching, and themes.

What is God revealing to you?

How can you apply this to your life today?

Prayer + Notes

DAY 11 | WATER

Pray over today's scripture, asking the Holy Spirit to lead you. Reread it and write what stands out in the space below.

2 KINGS 2:15-22

Observe the text for context, teaching, and themes.

What is God revealing to you?

How can you apply this to your life today?

Prayer + Notes

DAY 12 | WATER

Pray over today's scripture, asking the Holy Spirit to lead you. Reread it and write what stands out in the space below.

2 KINGS 3

Observe the text for context, teaching, and themes.

What is God revealing to you?

How can you apply this to your life today?

Prayer + Notes

DAY 13 | WATER

Pray over today's scripture, asking the Holy Spirit to lead you. Reread it and write what stands out in the space below.

PSALM 104:1-13

Observe the text for context, teaching, and themes.

What is God revealing to you?

How can you apply this to your life today?

Prayer + Notes

DAY 14 | WATER

Pray over today's scripture, asking the Holy Spirit to lead you. Reread it and write what stands out in the space below.

2 KINGS 5:1-14

Observe the text for context, teaching, and themes.

What is God revealing to you?

How can you apply this to your life today?

Prayer + Notes

DAY 15 | WATER

Pray over today's scripture, asking the Holy Spirit to lead you. Reread it and write what stands out in the space below.

PROVERBS 8:22-36

Observe the text for context, teaching, and themes.

What is God revealing to you?

How can you apply this to your life today?

Prayer + Notes

DAY 16 | WATER

Pray over today's scripture, asking the Holy Spirit to lead you. Reread it and write what stands out in the space below.

ISAIAH 12

Observe the text for context, teaching, and themes.

What is God revealing to you?

How can you apply this to your life today?

Prayer + Notes

DAY 17 | WATER

Pray over today's scripture, asking the Holy Spirit to lead you. Reread it and write what stands out in the space below.

ISAIAH 43:14-21

Observe the text for context, teaching, and themes.

What is God revealing to you?

How can you apply this to your life today?

Prayer + Notes

DAY 18 | WATER

Pray over today's scripture, asking the Holy Spirit to lead you. Reread it and write what stands out in the space below.

JEREMIAH 2:1-13

Observe the text for context, teaching, and themes.

What is God revealing to you?

How can you apply this to your life today?

Prayer + Notes

DAY 19 | WATER

Pray over today's scripture, asking the Holy Spirit to lead you. Reread it and write what stands out in the space below.

PSALM 107:23-32

Observe the text for context, teaching, and themes.

What is God revealing to you?

How can you apply this to your life today?

Prayer + Notes

DAY 20 | WATER

Pray over today's scripture, asking the Holy Spirit to lead you. Reread it and write what stands out in the space below.

EZEKIEL 47:1-12

Observe the text for context, teaching, and themes.

What is God revealing to you?

How can you apply this to your life today?

Prayer + Notes

DAY 21 | WATER

Pray over today's scripture, asking the Holy Spirit to lead you. Reread it and write what stands out in the space below.

MATTHEW 3

Observe the text for context, teaching, and themes.

What is God revealing to you?

How can you apply this to your life today?

Prayer + Notes

DAY 22 | WATER

Pray over today's scripture, asking the Holy Spirit to lead you. Reread it and write what stands out in the space below.

LUKE 5:1-11

Observe the text for context, teaching, and themes.

What is God revealing to you?

How can you apply this to your life today?

Prayer + Notes

DAY 23　|　WATER

Pray over today's scripture, asking the Holy Spirit to lead you. Reread it and write what stands out in the space below.

JOHN 2:1-12

Observe the text for context, teaching, and themes.

What is God revealing to you?

How can you apply this to your life today?

Prayer + Notes

DAY 24 | WATER

Pray over today's scripture, asking the Holy Spirit to lead you. Reread it and write what stands out in the space below.

JOHN 4:1-45

Observe the text for context, teaching, and themes.

What is God revealing to you?

How can you apply this to your life today?

Prayer + Notes

DAY 25 | WATER

Pray over today's scripture, asking the Holy Spirit to lead you. Reread it and write what stands out in the space below.

MARK 4:35-41

Observe the text for context, teaching, and themes.

What is God revealing to you?

How can you apply this to your life today?

Prayer + Notes

DAY 26 | WATER

Pray over today's scripture, asking the Holy Spirit to lead you. Reread it and write what stands out in the space below.

JOHN 9:1-12

Observe the text for context, teaching, and themes.

What is God revealing to you?

How can you apply this to your life today?

Prayer + Notes

DAY 27 | WATER

Pray over today's scripture, asking the Holy Spirit to lead you. Reread it and write what stands out in the space below.

MATTHEW 28:16-20

Observe the text for context, teaching, and themes.

What is God revealing to you?

How can you apply this to your life today?

Prayer + Notes

DAY 28 | WATER

Pray over today's scripture, asking the Holy Spirit to lead you. Reread it and write what stands out in the space below.

1 PETER 3:13-22

Observe the text for context, teaching, and themes.

What is God revealing to you?

How can you apply this to your life today?

Prayer + Notes

DAY 29 | WATER

Pray over today's scripture, asking the Holy Spirit to lead you. Reread it and write what stands out in the space below.

PSALM 114

Observe the text for context, teaching, and themes.

What is God revealing to you?

How can you apply this to your life today?

Prayer + Notes

DAY 30 | WATER

Pray over today's scripture, asking the Holy Spirit to lead you. Reread it and write what stands out in the space below.

REVELATION 22

Observe the text for context, teaching, and themes.

What is God revealing to you?

How can you apply this to your life today?

Prayer + Notes

insights + action

He who believes in Me, as the scripture said, "From his innermost being will flow rivers of living water".

JOHN 7:38

INSIGHTS | WATER

Let's revisit the last 30 days! Consider and meditate on your last 30 days spent in the Word of God and in prayer. Identify key insights about water from the Holy Spirit and capture them below.

ACTION | WATER

Now let's turn your insights into faith-based action steps!

Draw/write what comes to mind. Be as specific as possible.

> **TIP**: *For a starting point, review your life application notes from days 1–30.*

WATER

We are celebrating and praising God for the progress you have made in this journey. Whatever that may look like for you, you did it!

Redefine the full meaning of water in your own words, using your newly-gained, biblical insight.

Who can you share this with?

**From the end of the earth I call to You when my heart is faint;
Lead me to the rock that is higher than I.**

PSALM 61:2

Get your new journal at
hillseedjournals.com

www.ingramcontent.com/pod-product-compliance
Lightning Source LLC
Chambersburg PA
CBHW041309110526
44590CB00028B/4305